Fart Delivery Systems
Flatulence Product Catalog

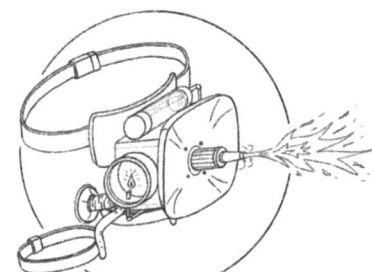
Delivery & Spreading

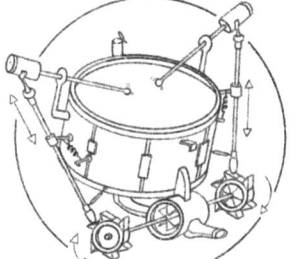
Musical Instruments

Automobile & Transports

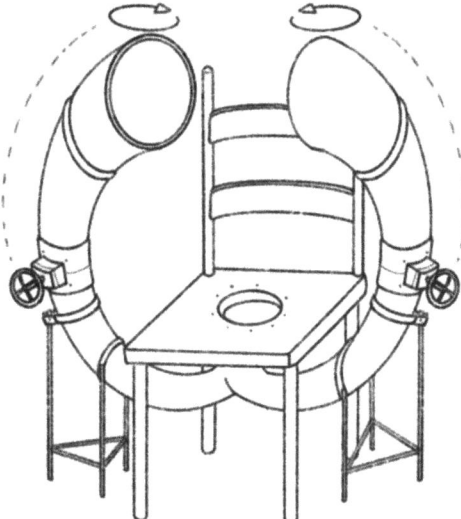

Cooking & Watching

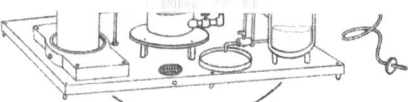
Books & Games

Home & Bathroom

Written & Illustrated by
Brad Gamwell

This book is dedicated to:
Poogie, my little potty humor engineer
&
Shnoose, my partner for ridiculous ideas

Special thanks to all family and friends who provided a buttload of flatulence related input...

and output.

Here's the part that nobody actually ever reads: the copyright jargon. Purple, Monkey, Dishwasher.

Believe it or not, this book is a work of fiction. All items, names and people are products of the author's weird imagination. Any resemblance to actual products, people or your mom is purely coincidental.

Copyright © 2022 Brad Gamwell

All rights reserved. No part of this book may be reproduced in any form without permission from the author. In other words, don't copy my work or you're a big stupid doodoo head.

First edition

ISBN 979-8-9865964-0-2

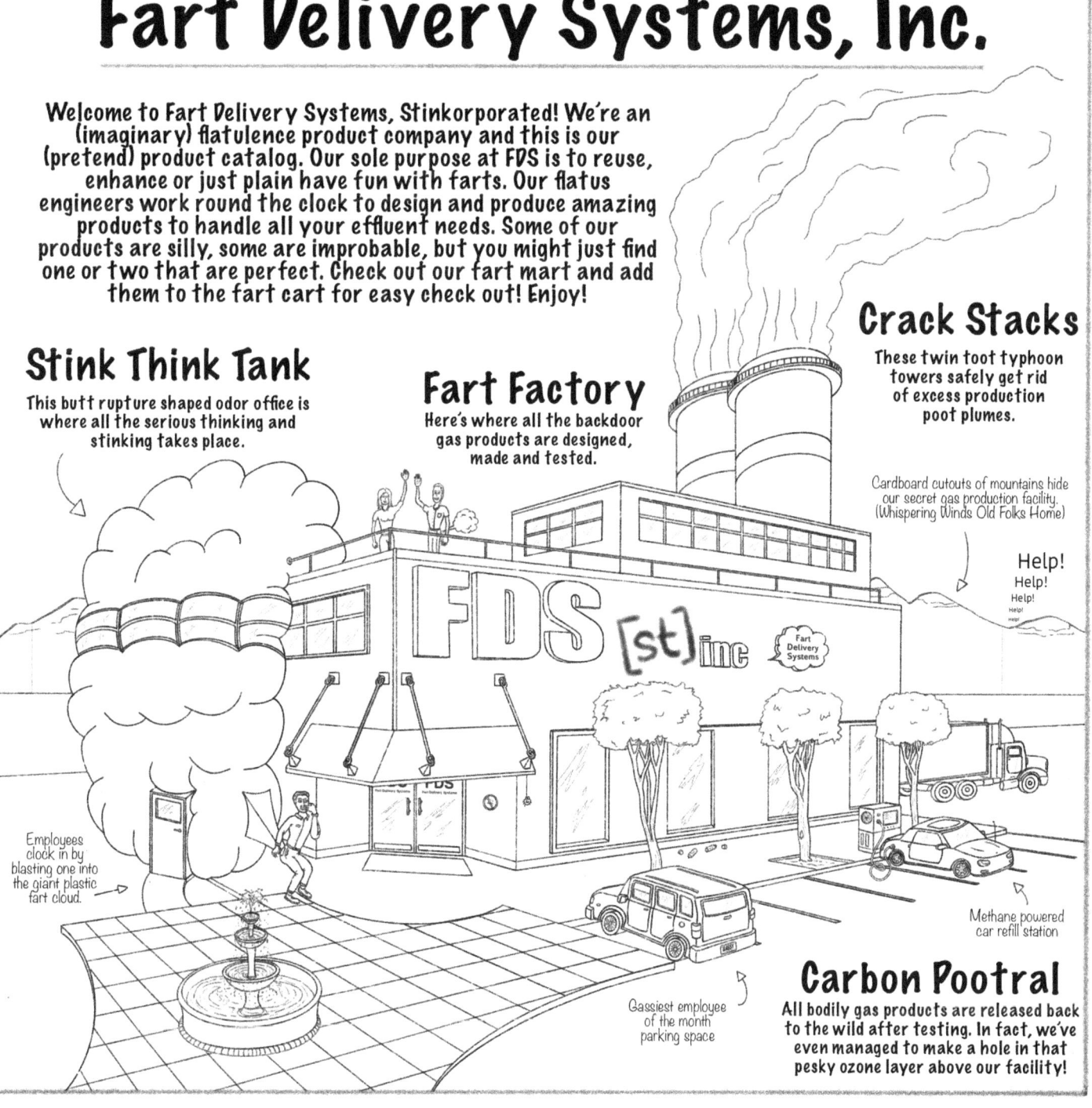

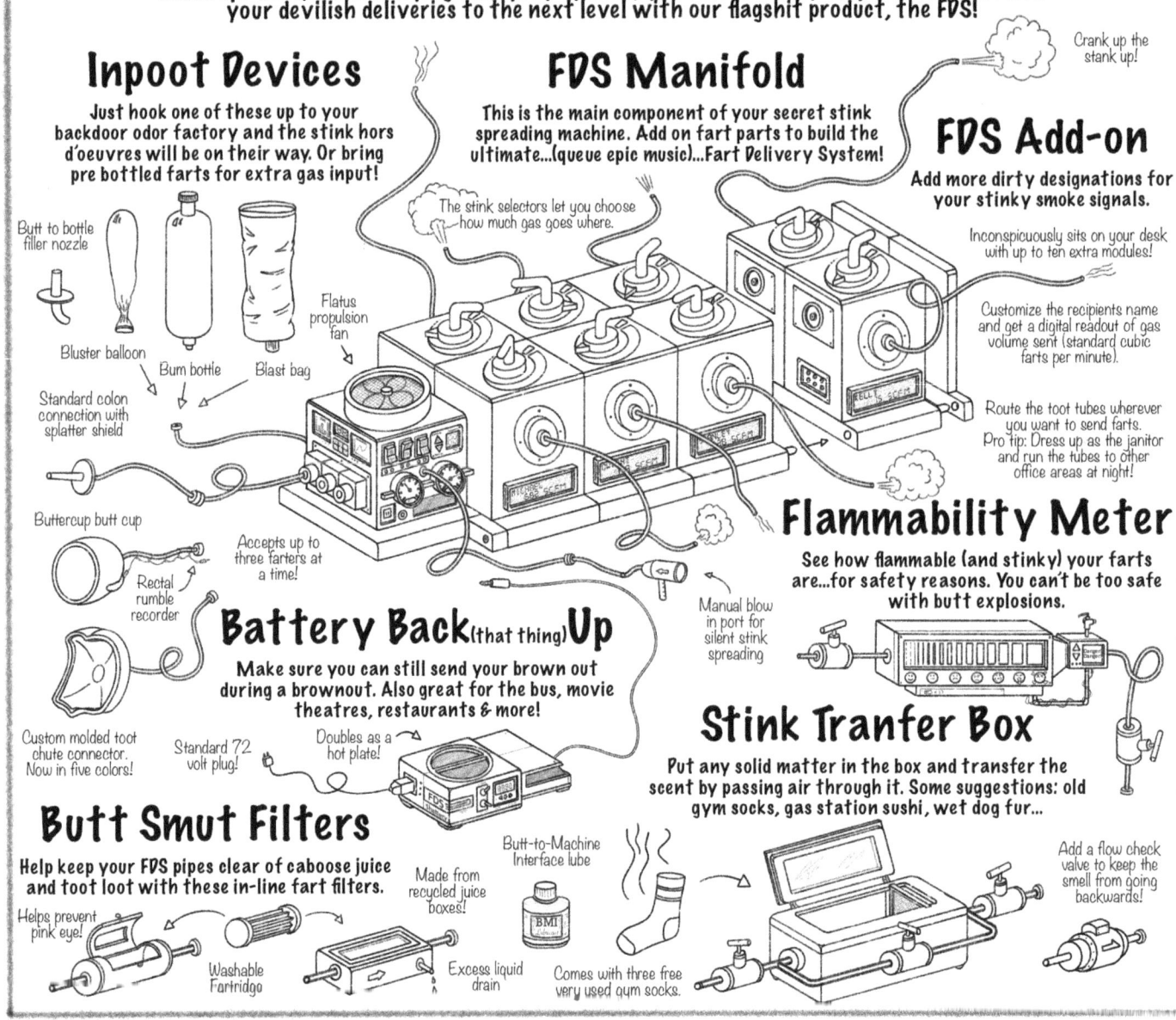

Flatulence Flaunting

Ever want to amplify your backdoor battle cry? Who actually ripped a juicier one, you or your wife? Did I just shart? These are real questions we face everyday. Well, discover here, the ultimate in fart amplification, stink measurements, rectal recordings and more. Next time you're a gassy Lassie, make sure to show off your blow off!

Backdoor Belts

Select one of these backside bandeaus to attach your gas gear to. Engineered to ensure a more secure strap-on when you get your crap-on.

Available in 3 upcycled styles:
- Premium - Used airplane seat belts
- Freemium - "Free" cargo shorts belt
- Oh-geemium - Garage sale bungee cord

Also works great for auto exotic assfixiation!

Shat Signals

Now you can easily tell if the small explosion between your legs also contained some dregs. Squirt alert!

The Foul Flag - A flag pops up to warn of poo particles in your pants.

The Flush Light - The stink strobe illuminates when it detects shorts sharts.

The Shart Tank - A water filled backpack that lets you "see" your butt bubbles. Blurrp! Built in check valve prevents enemas.

Flatus Flamethrower

Freely fling a five foot fart flame from your fundament! Great for taking care of that person that stands way too close to you in line.

Free barking spider lighter!

Flammable gas inlet. Made from recycled breast milk pumps.

Includes wet wipe dispenser

Premium bondage leather

Dubbed "The Dragon's Breath" by anti-gas officials. Requires a permit in Pew Hampshire.

Desktop Fartometers

Along with measuring all pant poot parameters, you can listen to your zipper zephyr over a loud speaker! Available in a single user desktop model or multiplayer floor model.

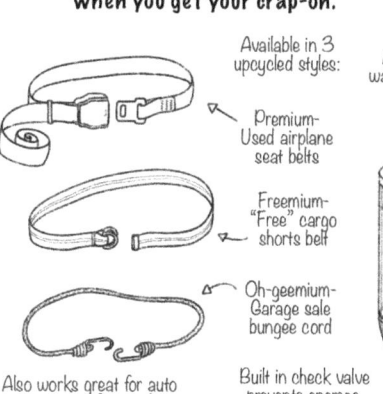

THHHUUURRRrrrroooo

Up to four players can go butt to butt with this typhoon toot tower. Just shove the stink sensor down your pants and blast away.

Comes with 2 wireless brown tooth industrial toxic gas sensors.

Squeeeaak

Exhaust port and heat sink fins double as a cup holder and taco stand!

Includes 10 fart games you can play with friends or against the computer!

"It's like a weather station... for your butt"
— Duke, Mishitigan

Clip-on Cloud Contraptions

These belt mounted mephitic meters make tooting a blast! Just run the stink sensor into your underwear and you're ready to blow. Link the modules together or add upgrade panels for extra functions.

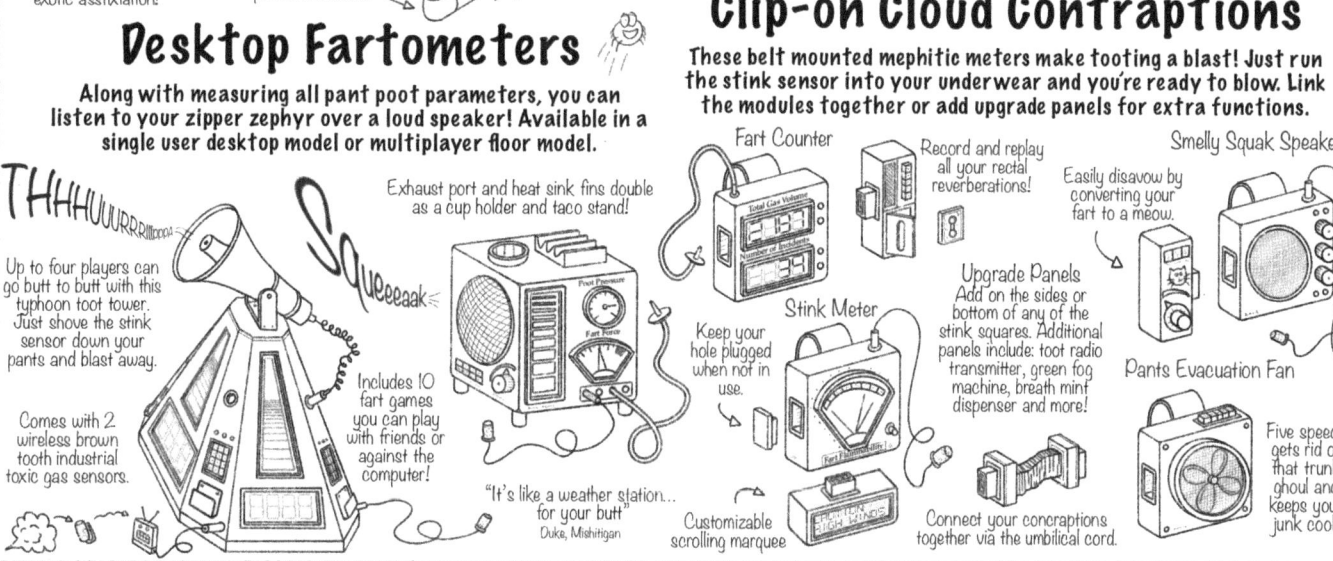

Fart Counter

Record and replay all your rectal reverberations!

Smelly Squak Speaker - Easily disavow by converting your fart to a meow.

Stink Meter - Keep your hole plugged when not in use.

Upgrade Panels - Add on the sides or bottom of any of the stink squares. Additional panels include: toot radio transmitter, green fog machine, breath mint dispenser and more!

Customizable scrolling marquee

Connect your concraptions together via the umbilical cord.

Pants Evacuation Fan - Five speeds gets rid of that trunk ghoul and keeps your junk cool!

Vile Domicile

According to some random, unverified statistics, people do 77% of their farting activities at home. 63% of that gas passing is done pantless. According to our mathemagicians, that's 140% of stink. That's why we have an entire division dedicated to home and bathroom butt bellows.

Stink Steambooth

This Toot filled Turkish bath completely saturates the user with a variety of odious odors. Repoovenate your skin, alleviate assma, or keep weirdos away due to your unusual scent.

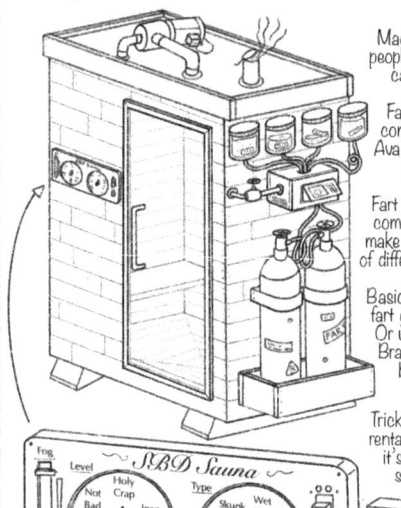

Made for 1-2 people...but you can fit 7.

Fart flavor concentrate. Available in 18 types.

Fart fog mixing computer. Can make a crap load of different scents.

Basic unscented fart gas bottles. Or upgrade to Brazilian butt bottles!

Trick your friends or rental customers that it's just a normal steam room...

C-CRAP Machine

Stop snoring and farting in the bed at night! This machine saves marriages and sheets.

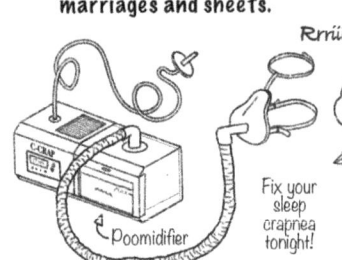

Poomidifier

Fix your sleep crapnea tonight!

Ass-orted Alarmclocks

Enjoy waking up to the sounds and smells of turd bypass air as it gently wafts across your face.

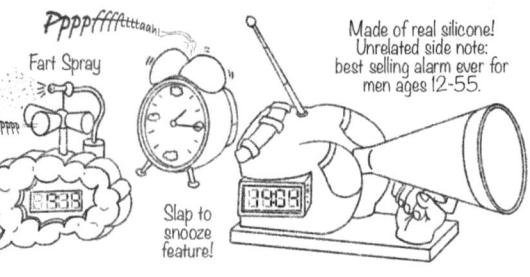

Ppppfffttttaahh

Fart Spray

Rrrüüiippp

Made of real silicone! Unrelated side note: best selling alarm ever for men ages 12-55.

Slap to snooze feature!

Butthole Balm

Keep your flatus whistle from getting chapped with our sphincter salve.

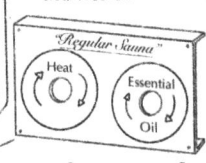

Hot Air Hand Dryer

This comically shaped, butt hand dryer makes drying yourself a blast!

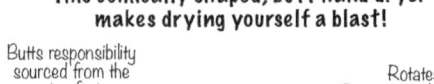

Butts responsibly sourced from the sex toy factory test reject bin. Available in firm, jiggly and saggy.

Rotates up to dry your face.

Pesky 3rd prong already removed!

Convenient 6" power cord

Stank Tank

Just like old farts, wheel this portable tank of toots around breathing in gassy goodness.

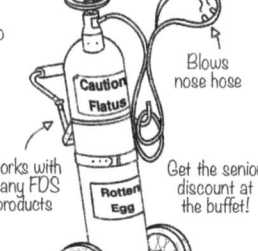

Flatulence Audio Receiver/ Transmitter Box

Blows nose hose

Works with many FDS products

Get the senior discount at the buffet!

10x8 brown tooth microphones

Humans: Underwear mounted
Animals: Tail mounted

Home Fart Scoreboard

The wall mounted home electronic toot tabulator keeps track of up to eight flatulators. With five built in fart games, you'll have hours of fart fun!

See who farts the most or least! The system measures number, volume, and noise of rectal releases. Includes a butthole shocking fart scold mode.

Fart Fragrances

Smell your worst with these shart scented body sprays. True eau de toilet.

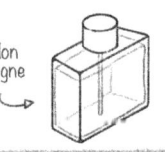
Colon cologne

Putrid perfume

Stink Sharing

Take your stench spreading to the next level with these innovative impolite products. You're covered for remote cropdusting, friendly fart fights, and smell symphonies. We've even updated the ole fart under the covers gag. Sharing is caring!

Dutch Oven Pro

This undercover under-the-covers fart sharing blanket makes making a toot tent super simple!

- Connect your pjs via the wind tunnel!
- Non-breathable fabric keeps the farts in longer!
- Elastic bands keep the farts from going out the wrong hole.
- The blankets edges are weighted to throw over people more easily.
- Magnetic snaps along the sides automatically connect in place so the person can't escape.

Butt Bomb

Set the timer, then place this stink ball into any random object. Just some ideas: wife's pillow, boss's office, kid's backpack...

- Choose classic timer or time intervals. Then, choose fluff, blast, or release all. Three full hours of stank!
- Fake fast food bags: Booger King, Windy's, SickDonald's, Dairy Queef, Little Cheesers, & Taco Smell.
- Fluff stuffed animals: Shat Cat, Fog Dog & Smelephant

Malodorous Mailer

Use this sealed stink sender to share your gas with suspecting or unsuspecting people! Distance can't keep you afart.

- Triple seal
- Prepaid, discreet, padded envelope
- RC car (Remote Cropduster)

Famous People Poots

Our specially trained pooparazzi follow celebrities around and catch their farts so you can have the smell of success too.

Special odor order: Up-Chuck Norris.

Leofarto DiCrapio, Brad Armpitt, Lady Gag-ah!, Tom Poos, Farti B, Tom Stanks, Smel Gibson, Shat Damon, Chris Shat, Smellen DeGeneres, Dolly Farton, Elon Musky

Hear Rear Here Chair

Sit down, relax and listen to the pure, unadulterated sounds of your back door bellows. Rotate the brown horn so others can enjoy the musty music.

- Double horn for brown surround sound!
- Turn any chair into an excrete seat with a DIY [butt]hole saw! 3 hole sizes: large, medium and glory.

Foul Flowers

Place the fart smell impregnator into any vase with flowers and voilà, instant gross smelling pooquet.

- The stink puck keeps flowers alive and nasty for 17 weeks!
- Pro tip: flowers are expensive so just borrow them from your neighbors yard.

Toot Travel Translator

Translates only fart related words and phrases into 161 different languages. Great for traveling abroad or when visiting the local taco truck.

"I farted!" → "Me tiré un pedo!"

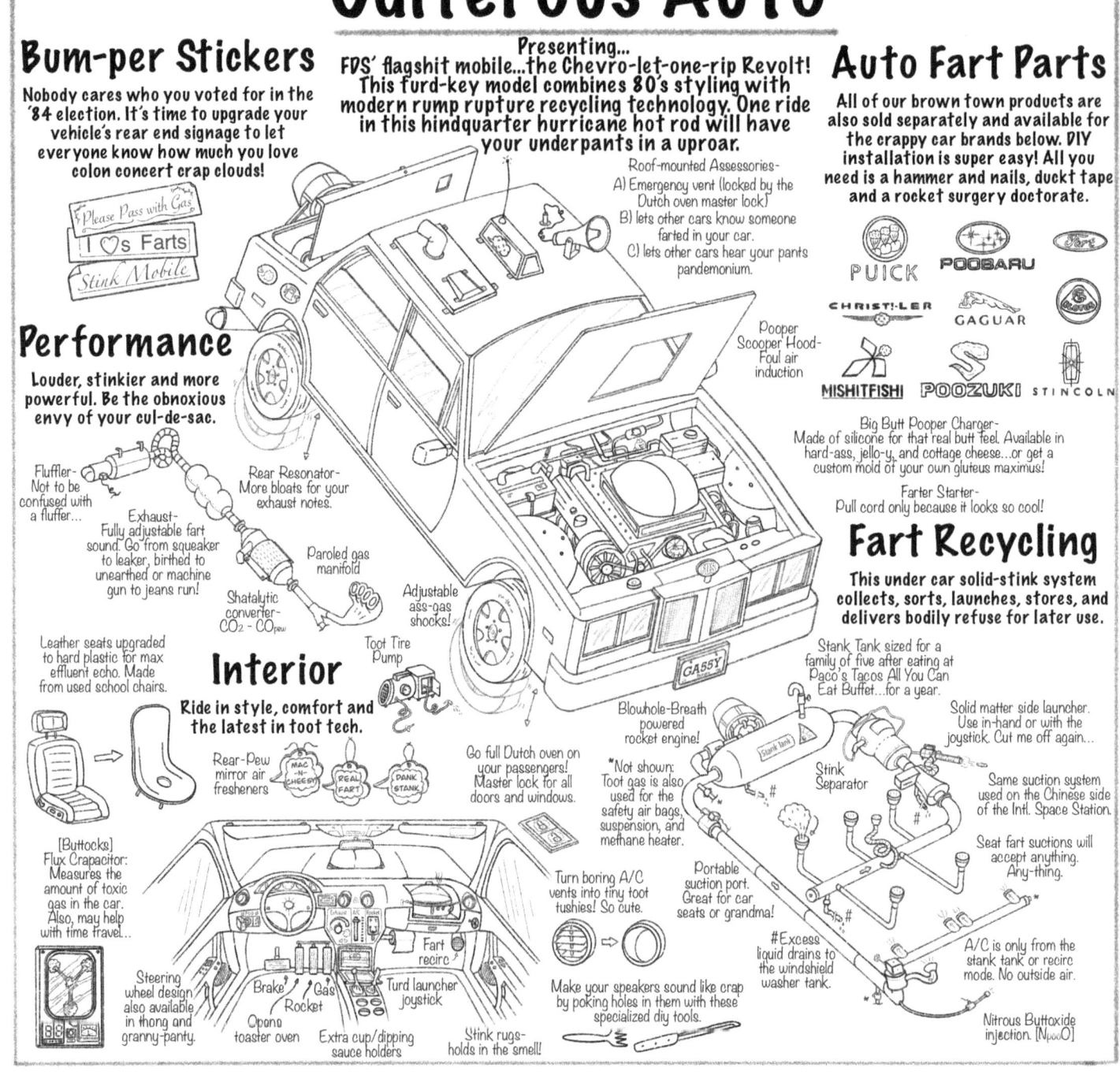

Toot Transports

Instead of wasting farts and destroying the ozone layer, why not use your own personal back door energy releases to move yourself around? Our selection of personal poot propulsion products will knock your socks off.

Pooter Scooter

Putter around town on this silent but medley stink sled.

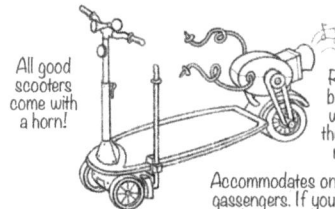

All good scooters come with a horn!

Recycled music box parts mixed with farts make the most beautiful musty melody.

Accommodates one or two gassengers. If you want to ride, you must provide.

Butt Blast Bike

A puff powered pedal propulsion pedelec bicycle. Period. No, no, no... like a punctuation mark, not a menstrual cycle, you freakin weirdo. Jeez-sus.

Air activated accordion acceptor ensures a gas-tight comfortable chair connection.

Not gassy? Strap on some spare stank storage!

"Super easy to use. It's just like riding a bicycle..." Luke Geezson, Arizona

Hot Ass-Air Balloon

Baby swing stink seat swivels 360 degrees for breathtaking poos and views!

Available with a cockpit for men or dockpit for women.

Featuring a personalized, super sealed, rubber coated, tighty whitey style crotch cockpit. Float with the clouds using you own floating clouds.

Poogo Stick

An anal air assisted, spring loaded jumping stick. Eat it Commander Keen.

Butt blast belt included!

Every bounce auto compresses your gas into the fart tank.

Then the user can manually activate the bottom blast nozzles.

Hiney Hovercraft

Glide over land and water on a cushion of anal air from downwardly directed flatulence fans.

Kills grass faster than a slip and slide in summer!

Bring the swamp smell with you wherever you go!

Crack Jet Pack

Now you can be the Rear Rocketier! 3, 2, 1, Blast off! Save the day!

Start a sky writing business with this crack smoke stack!

Comes with chewing gum to plug any leaks.

Smelicopter

This go-go gadget helicrapter is easier to assemble than an IKEA bookshelf and doesn't charge you for a carry-on bag like some flights (Poo-nited Airlines).

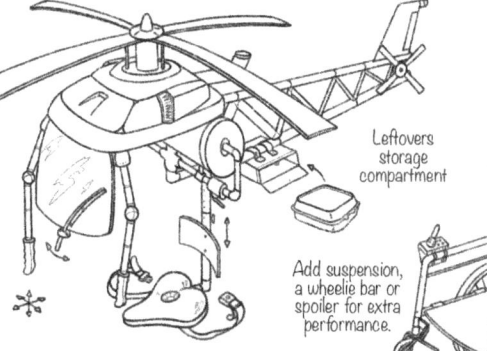

Leftovers storage compartment

Probably requires some sort of license to fly this crap contraption. Check with the (FFAA) federal fart air administration.

Air Wheelchair

Why not put grandma's bountiful bottom blurts to good use? Plus now you won't have to fight those fake handicap people for the only charged cart at Wally World.

Standard stink electric version

Upgraded raunchy rocket version

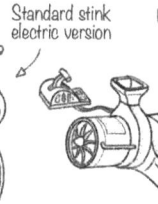

Add suspension, a wheelie bar or spoiler for extra performance.

Add either poot package to any old wheel chair!

Floater Motor

Bloaterize anything that moves! Make a blow row boat (not like Wallstreet wolf style), windy wagon, or even fart go cart!

Literally made of stuff from the recycling center.

With enough friends you could make an air-plane!

Prat Whid Shiterature

Check out our collection of rump rumbling related writing from some of the most famous whimsical wind writers. From Troubletooting to Cropdusting, Ripe Jokes to How-Poo guides, there's something for everybody.

Pharto Al-bums
Proudly display your stinkiest moments! Includes diy scratch-n-sniff squares. Also great for crapbooking.

Gaseous Guidance
Gas guides for all things fart related. Be sure to check out our Pootube Channel for some sweet shideos.

Add your own pages of gassy goodness!

Bloat Note Taking
The smudge proof paper is great for jotting down your daily releases!

Electronic Phonics
This interactive book series helps teach kids and other illiterates that it's ok to toot the tushy train whistle sometimes.

Follow Puff, the farting, self conscious train engine as he learns about life, love and lettin 'em rip.

Graphic Gas Novels
Follow the airy adventures of your favorite pooper heroes and villains!

First appearance: "The Gas Stoppers"!

Adventyour Gas
Fart filled tales of action ripe with septic swamp swagger.
Genres: Steamy Punk, My-Sigh-Fi & Fantasy.

Fouling will keep you on the edge of your toilet seat!
— Ben Dover, Chicago Times

Decompression Expression
Explore creative ways to open your odoriferous orifice. Not for the faint of fart.

Pocket poot guide

Just Released: Feel Good Reads
Funny stories, joke books and fart product catalogs.

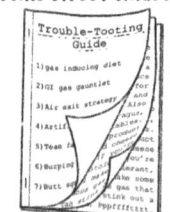

Social and Ethical Flatulence
Delve deep into the moral and ethical questions surrounding gas release. Should I be uncomfortable or them? Will it even smell? Why now?! Everything you thought you knew about lower lamentations was wrong...

Flatus Applications for Teaching
Ever wonder how fast a fart was traveling? Or how to maximize rear reverberations? Learn how to solve pressing, real world flatulence problems.

Cropdusting Collection
Learn the stealthy (f)art of passing gas, maximizing it's spread and avoiding detection. Become a legend...

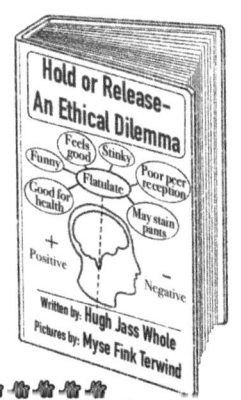
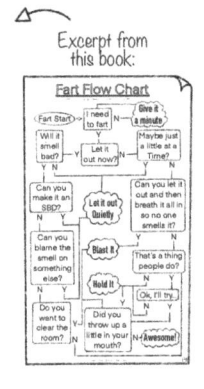
Excerpt from this book:

"Mind and bowels blown"
Dr Adam Gaswell, Fartologist PhD

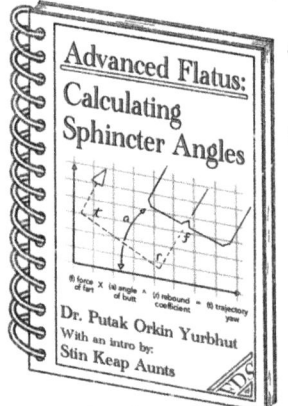

This book: Discover how to perfectly position your throttle valve to achieve maximum rear detonation velocity.

Also in this series:
Ideal Butt Cheek Positions for Classic Blasts

This book: Learn how to perfectly premeditate poot proliferation. Make a crap-map, time your crime, and even double down with a fartner partner! They won't even know what just (s)hit them. Legend...... dairy.

Also in this series:
Best Places to Cropdust & Cropdusting for Dum dums

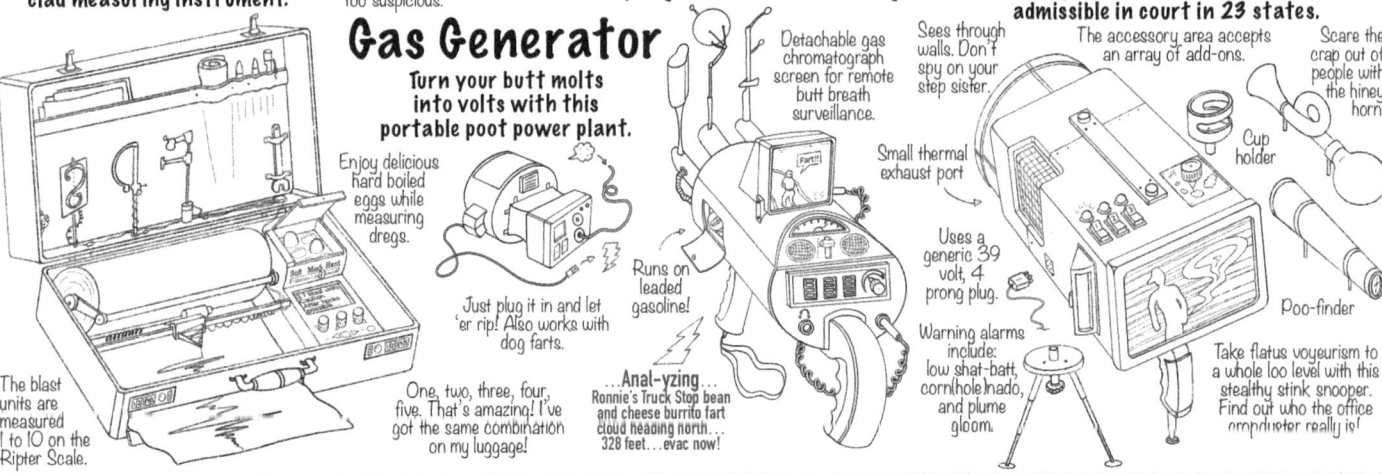

Reek Removal

So, we're not really sure why people would want to remove beautiful smelling butt wind. Apparently, some people do. These products remove farts and neutralize odors. But don't worry, the removed aft air afterburners can be easily recycled!

Fart Removal Header

This ceiling mounted stink suction header removes unpleasant odors via super stretchy flex hoses. Great for bedrooms, conference rooms, Mexican restaurants and more!

Discrete Tweet Delete Seat

Let out those derrière devils with confidence and no one will know. Transports your pants poots quickly away from nosy nostrils.

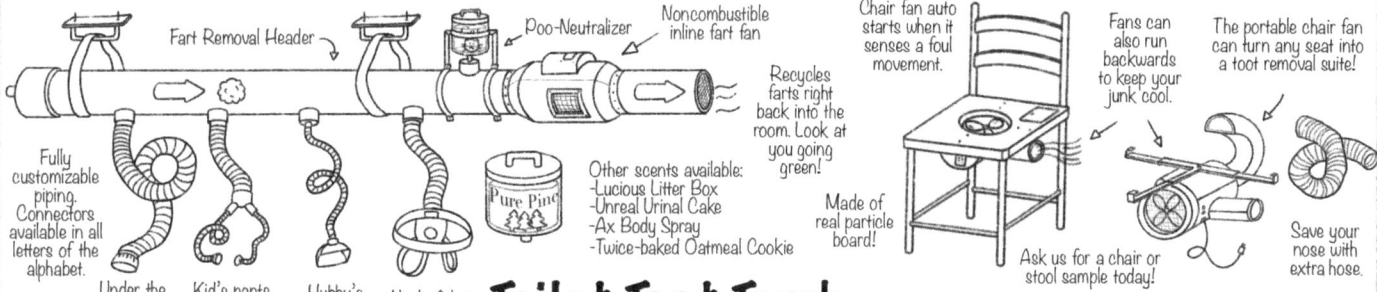

Butt Leaf Blower

You're sure to get extra high fives from other neighborhood dads with this hilarious tool shed upgrade.

Toilet Toot Torch

Let's face it, the amount of gas YOU release while taking the Browns to the Super Bowl is too much for a standard exhaust fan. Time to light it up!!

Patootie Mufflers

Not ready to come out of the proverbial gas closet yet? Well, hide all your stink, stank and stunk with these cool looking concraptions.

Caboose Cover Spray

Masking a fart with another weird smell usually doesn't work. But you can try.

Flatus Liquid Concentrate Extractor

Just wheel this bad boy wherever farts are present and start making brown gold!

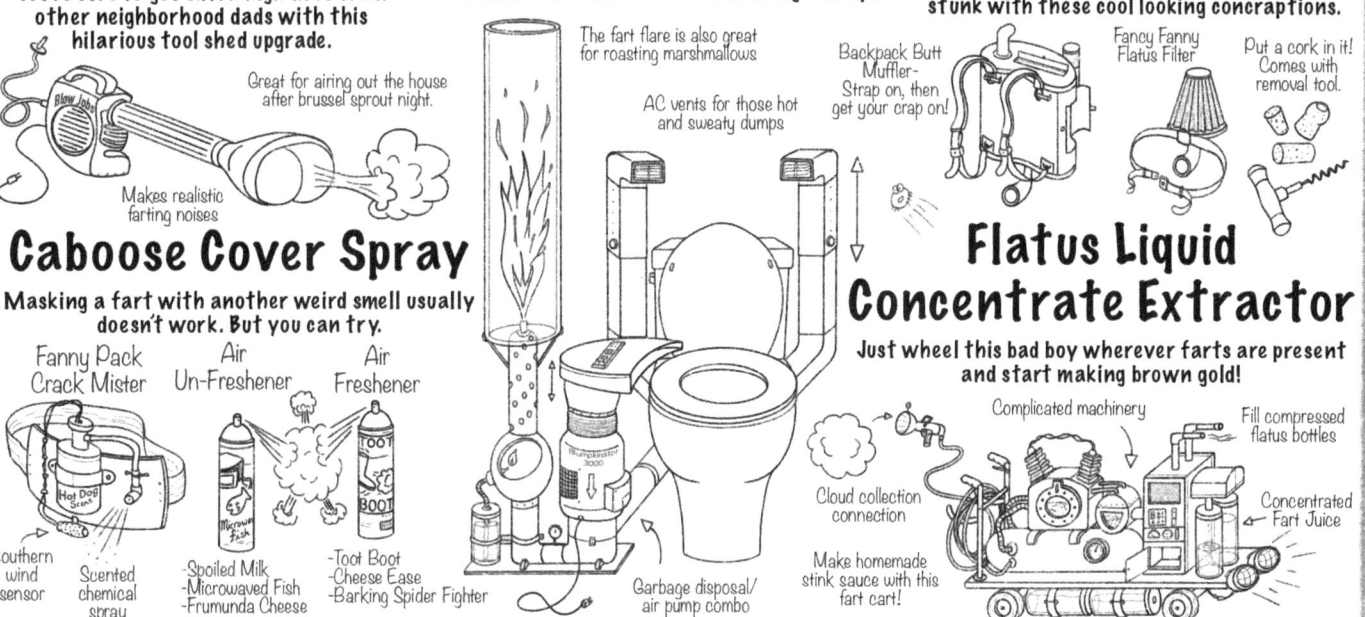

Obscene Cusine

Way before electricity or even fire was discovered, cave humans used to cook with flatus. We've modernized fart cooking products so you can enjoy them in your home. So gather family and friends to start a new tradition of sharing warm stories and farts this year! Bon crappétit!

Fart Food Steamer

Slowly cook delicious food in your own personal seasoning. Comes with a "Y" splitter so you can cook with a friend. The optional clear lid lets you see your food simmering in tasty toot juice!

Great for anonymous potluck lunches. No one will suspect they are literally tasting your tookus toots.

Comes with a free stink mitt!

Connect to our bed fart removal system to continue cooking all night while you sleep!

Unlock nuclear mode! For serious users only. Requires FDS president's permission and thirty minutes of specialized training.

Fluff Puff Pastry Maker

Taste the warm tangy air rush into your mouth as you bite into these homemade humdinger pockets. Mouth and eye watering.

Make dough → Flatten into a circle → Fold → Fill with farts and bake!

Pump your rump thump into actual air biscuits!

Also great for filling pool floaties!

Crème Poôlée Torch

Easily make fart flamed desserts with subtle notes of half digested brussels sprouts. Top with fart infused whipped cream.

Great for rip it whip-its!

Also comes in extra thick or fermented

*naturally brown

Fart flame output

Always use caution when releasing gas around fire.

Brown dot sights included

Duff Dish Dryer

Quickly air dry washed dishes using your built in patootie breeze. From underwear to tableware, this crack rack dries and shines in no time!

Slight browning of dishes may occur...

Also great for a face and hand dryer. You'll never buy a towel again!

The butt burp bladder disperses hot air to dry your dishes.

Chair Fryer

Just have a seat, slide out a couple of greasy air snakes and you've got fabulous fart fried food!

Fart french fries, butt breaded burritos, tooty tater tots & more!

The stool stool comes in medium, large & yo mama sizes.

Excess juice drain.

Extra gas input

Fart Smoker Grill

Expertly grill bbq badonkadonk burgers, fart fajitas or stinky steaks. Extra gas stank tank ethically produced at the local old folks home.

Don't forget the fart flipper and toot tongs.

Rust and crust proof coating

Industrial fart igniter

Compressed Flatus

Comes with three inputs but it can take up to six users at once.*

*Caution: limit of six excludes lactose intolerant users who just went on a dairy binge.

Cooking Shiterature

Liktuff Art Daylie Presents: Cooking with Gas, from your Ass
Illustrations by: Holeek Rapyouse Tink
P-U-SA Today Best Smeller

Stink Drink

These sick-wid liquid devices can be used to make the perfect poo brew, deuce juice, smelixir or even a fartini. Enjoy the taste of fresh, barista bumdinger beverages, right in your own home!

Caboose Booze
Butt bubbly, p-u brew, sicker liquor and windy wine; let's get this par-tay started!

Fart Soda Maker
Enjoy the refreshing taste of fart infused flavor with every slurp. With each blast you'll enjoy crispy butt bubbles that dance across your tongue.

- Glass is dishwasher safe, but we do not recommend washing it in order to keep the flavor sealed in.
- Check valve to keep bubbles flowing the right way.
- Three total toot taps

Fart Soda Bottler
Now you can take your fart infused soda anywhere you want to go. Great for parties (farties)!

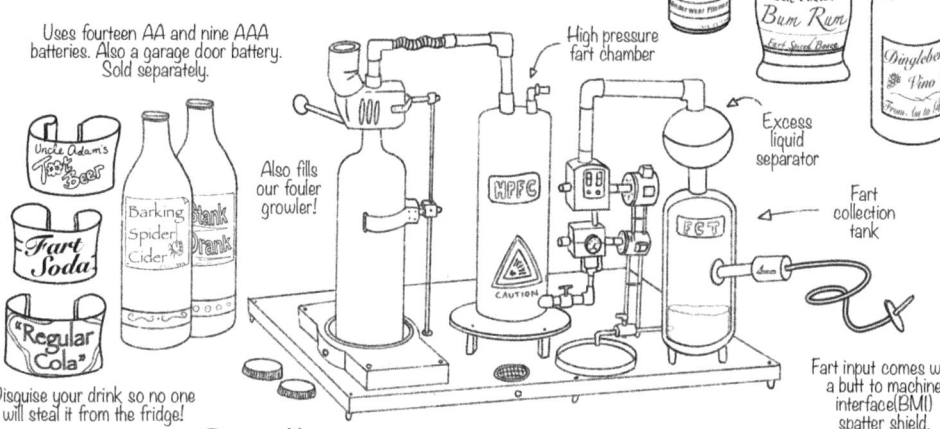

- Uses fourteen AA and nine AAA batteries. Also a garage door battery. Sold separately.
- Custom fart soda labels
- Also fills our fouler growler!
- High pressure fart chamber
- Excess liquid separator
- Fart collection tank
- Fart input comes with a butt to machine interface (BMI) spatter shield.
- Disguise your drink so no one will steal it from the fridge!
- Monogram bottle caps, now in Russian.

Crappuccino Machine
Start your day off right with a steamy cup of butt Java and frothy fart milk. And way cheaper than your local StarCrooks Coffee shop!

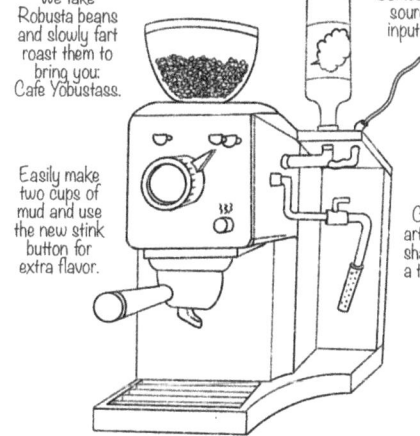

- We take Robusta beans and slowly fart roast them to bring you: Cafe Yobustass.
- Comes with responsibly sourced fart gas or input your signature taste.
- Easily make two cups of mud and use the new stink button for extra flavor.
- Create latte fart art then add some shart sprinkles for a truly phew-nique experience!

Tainted Tea
This gut gas green tea might just actually make you turn green!

- Mmmm! Find your favorite fart flavor.
- Give your wife, boss or even a stranger a nice teabag!

Fart Enhancing Products
Do you want to clear that boring meeting out with another "sewer leak" so you can get to lunch early? Or how about have your daughter think a unicorn just left magical glitter kisses in the air? Well, we've got you covered...from the front because...you know.

- Get the extra volume and stink you need to destroy your coworkers next taco Tuesday!
- Take crop dusting to a whole new level by adding color or thickness to your next air biscuit.

- Ass-orted glitter and scents.

"Is that fresh cookies I smell? Nope, that's my new fart scent. And here comes the glitter!"
-Lu G, from Gassachusetts

PUsical Instruments

Oh, playing music with your bare butt is glorious! Now imagine adding a finely tuned instrument to that toot chute! We've got (wood) Wind, (br) Ass, Stinky Strings, and of course, Percussion models available.

Butt Tuba
Imagine the sound (and smell) of a mating walrus mixed with a pissed off Tauntaun. Then add a flamethrower. Pure awesomeness!

- Hit that brown note every time! Maybe, just bring extra shorts.
- Don't forget to buckle up for safety! Gas leaks are no fun.
- The chain pull toot torch burns off explosive gases and also just looks freaking sweet!
- Clean out butt buildup with the shitspit spigot.

Toot Flute
Dubbed the sphincter snorkel, this dainty girl is rumored to be in the next Willy Wonka and the Chocolate Factory movie!

- Easily breaks down for transport. Play at the park, in the break room or even a buddy's bachelor party!
- Impress everyone at your next class reunion with your new musical skills. They're sure to let you in the cool kids club now.

Didgeripoo
This wind aerophone's inspiration is from halfway around the world where the toilets flush backwards. Enjoy the sounds from down unda!

- Breath in...squeeze out...Take circular breathing to a whole new level.
- Just squat, relax and feel the sounds flow out of you.

Gas-Bagpipes
This instrument already sounds like a prepubescent boy asking a date out to the school dance. Well, it's time to graduate to manhood with this hot air powered tune thrower. Pure bass straight from your ace.

- Fart flags let you make sure the right people are standing downwind
- Fart fluid drain valve
- Extra gas bag for after your visit to the taco truck.
- Now, you actually have a good reason to not wear underwear under your kilt.

Shitar
This sit down, gas powered stringed music player will knock your listeners dead. Farts collect in the body and then are released by finger switches to vibrate the strings beautifully.

- Comes with a free G string. That one always seems to get the dirtiest.
- Don't let the rosewood fool you into thinking it smells nice. It doesn't.
- Shy about playing pantsless? Try the optional crotch curtain. Rain and stain proof.
- Foot holders keep you firmly planted while ripping out some sick shitar solos!

Stinky Trombone
Not to be confused with the rusty trombone, this hiney horn delivers crisp butt-ery notes and airy floats.

- Play it up high or down low.
- Highly configurable! Add more horns for more scorns. The extra butt piece allows smellow musicians to chime in.
- Attach a butt belt here
- Works with most other FDS devices.

Smelly Snare Drum
With our cutting-edge crap to rap technology, now you can literally march to the beat of your own drum.

- Blow off valve
- This dirty drum has lots of moving parts. Be sure to keep it well oiled or it'll become well soiled.
- Tunable up to 622 backdoor beats per minute.

Rectal Recorder
We've combined the already most annoying instrument with obnoxious odors! Great for the grandkids. Their parents will hate you more than if you got them a drum set.

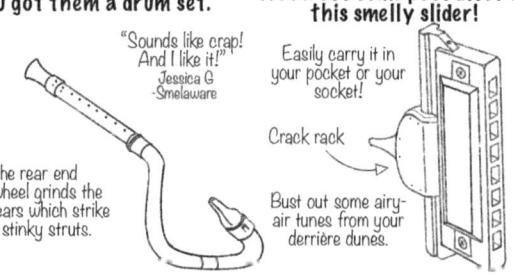

- "Sounds like crap! And I like it!" Jessica G -Smelaware
- The rear end rotowheel grinds the gas gears which strike the stinky struts.

Vertical Fartmonica
Crank out some poos blues on this smelly slider!

- Easily carry it in your pocket or your socket!
- Crack rack
- Bust out some airy-air tunes from your derrière dunes.

Blast Tube
Our proprietary tube design forces the release away from the user while giving it maximum echo. Made in house, from 100% recycled material.

- A lot of sit down time was needed to make this product.
- Blast tube mini! So cute. Sooo stinky.

Airy Attire

Our line of crappy clothes not only look and smell great, but they're also 100% fully flatus functional! Share your gas gracefully, easily connect to other poot products and even show off your blow off.

Winter Cr-Apparel

This recently paroled cold weather wear uses your own body's butt blasts to warm and insulate the wearer. Add beaver fur lining for extra warmth!

Shat Hat — Reservoir tip stores stink for later. Also has a slow release function.

Barf Scarf — Wraps you in a cozy layer of warm butt gas. Bonus mode: when someone borrows your scarf, it locks around their neck and slowly releases stink air in their face!

Shittin Mittens — Easily direct toots toward someone else. Try blasting someone while shaking hands!

Rear Head Gear

Mixing farts with hats made about as much sense as mixing corn and peanut butter. But we did it and it was delicious! And we made the hats too.

Bumbrero — Goes great with a Rauncho Poncho!

Yugoslavian Fart Helmet — This type of smelmet was originally used by WWII sailors as a form of gambling.

Propel-her Hat — A bean powered beanie!

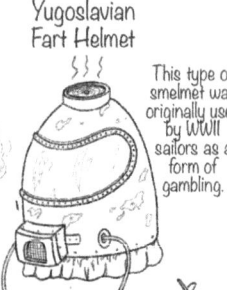

Bottom Bottoms

Normal pants just get in the way of effectively passing gas. Not to mention how much the sound suffers with your fart box all smothered in underwear. Well frustrated flatulaters, try these on for size!

Wind Tunnel Pants — Lets your brew pass right through. Also easy access to connect to other fart products. Available in full length strength, snorts shorts and breeze capris.

Steam Streamers — SBDs are almost impossible with this intestinal vent warning system.

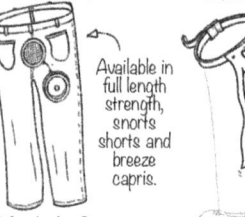

Manhole Cover — Avoid indecent exposure charges because your brown eye winked at someone.

Rubber Underwear — Air tight, penetration free, universal gas connection.

 Crap Flap

Toot Suits

There's always someone who wants to take their fart wear to the next level. Here ya go...

Sauna Stink Suit — Toot transfer tube: connect to other suits to wear, share and compare. Triple sealed at the ankles to prevent gas leaks.

Plume Costume — Mini airlock to transfer items in or out of the toot suit. Built in sneaker leaker and turd wrangler apparati. Made from 100% recycled abandoned gym locker room underwear.

Poo Shoes

We've figured a way to convert the kinetic energy of walking into amusing flatus sounds. Full credit to grandma for all her walking farts.

Toot Boots — Built in self inflating whoopie cushions.

Loaf Loafers — Fart impregnated leather makes them smell as bad as they look.

Squeaker Sneakers — No laces needed. Your gas fills the shoe's bladders for a secure fit. Gas cushions. Blow off valve.

Clothes Fart Steamer

Keep your clothes looking snazzy and smelling nasty with this self supplied stink steamer!

Saturation bag. Removes wrinkles! Not for your face. Get that fresh cesspool smell soaked into any of your clothes.

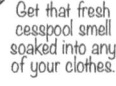

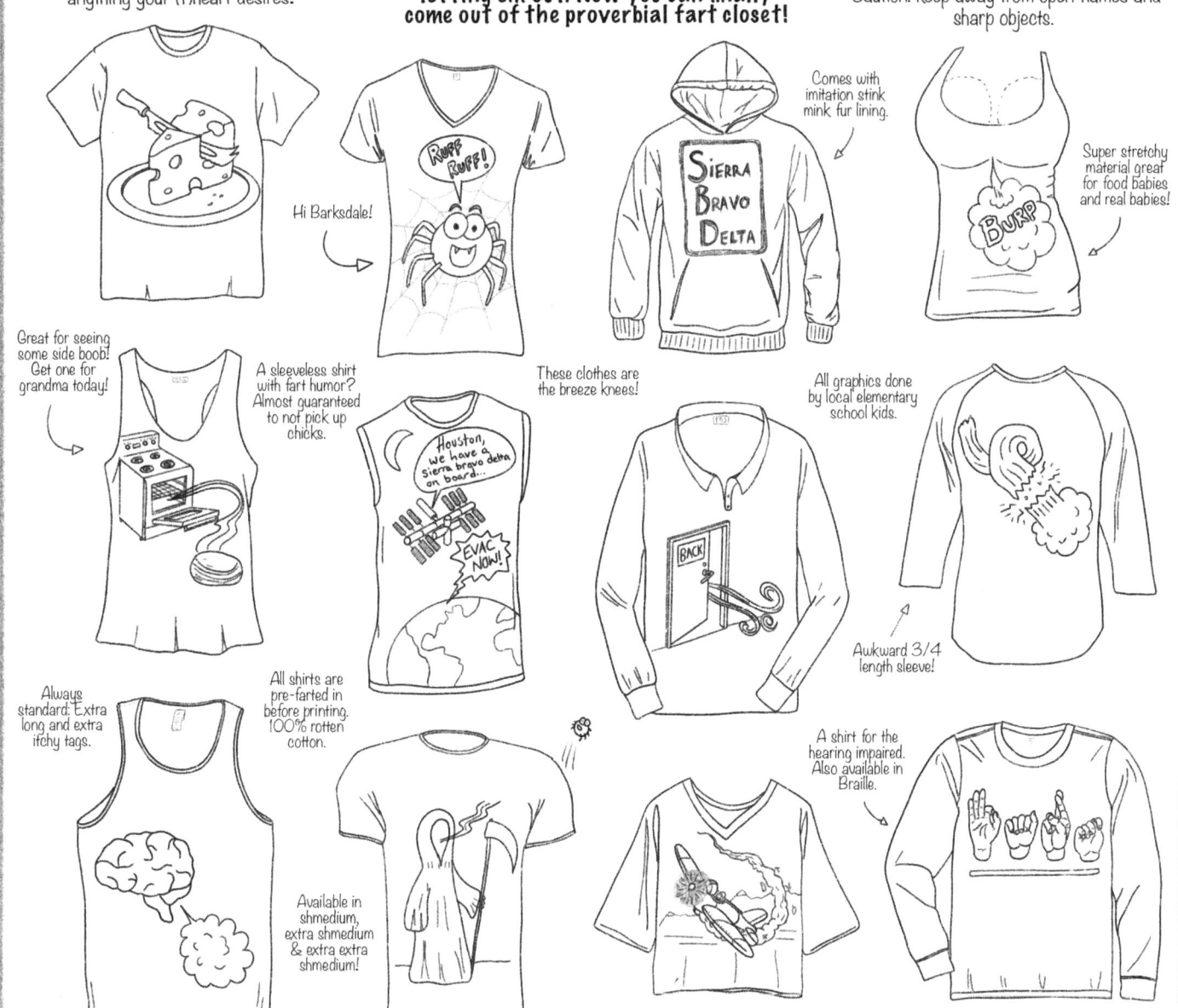

Cloud Compooters

Each advanced flatus computer is custom made based on the users needs and the fact that it's made from random e-waste from the local recycling center. All computers assembled by the local forth grade computer club. (This makes profits super high for these items. Editor: remove this line before publishing.)

Model:
Deflaties 80's

This super pooper computer combines all the sweetest, state of the fart eighties toy tech into one all powerful fart centric machine!

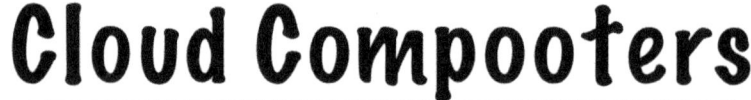

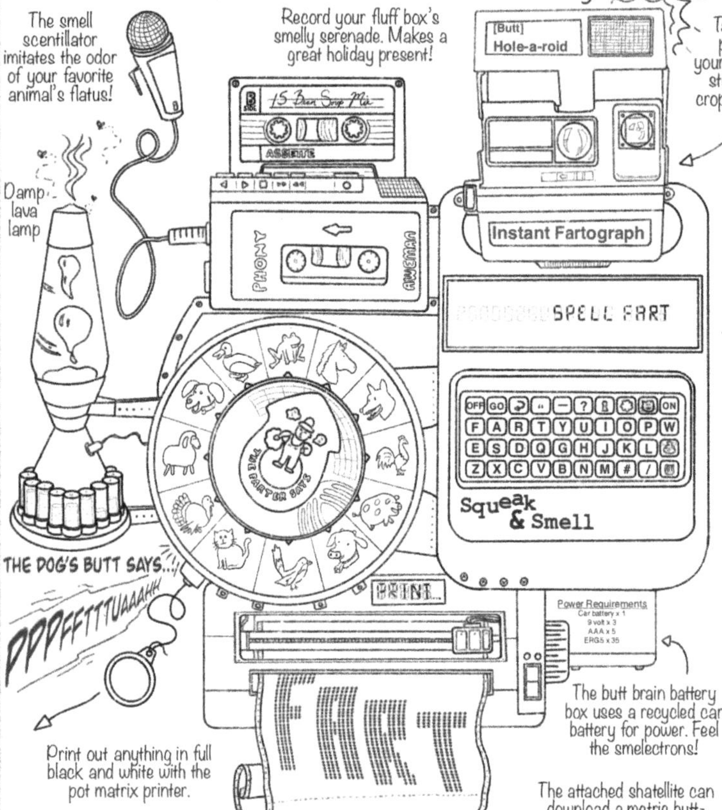

Model:
Immersion Gamer Pod

Play the latest video games while bathing in your own farts. The fastest C-PU in town!

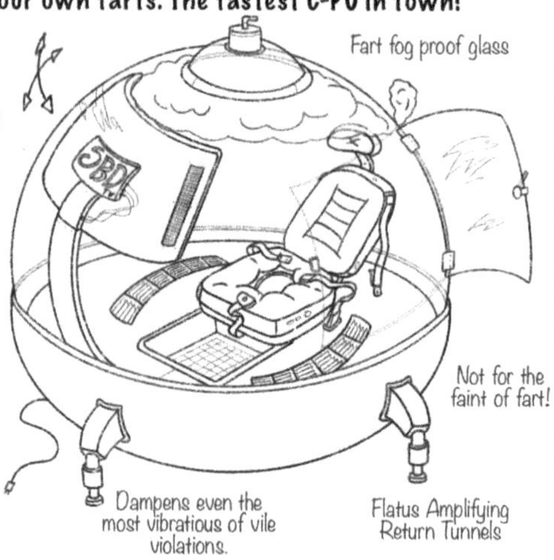

Model:
Fartificial Intelligence

Upload your cloud to the cloud, perform advanced fart calculations, or even... take-over-the-humans...

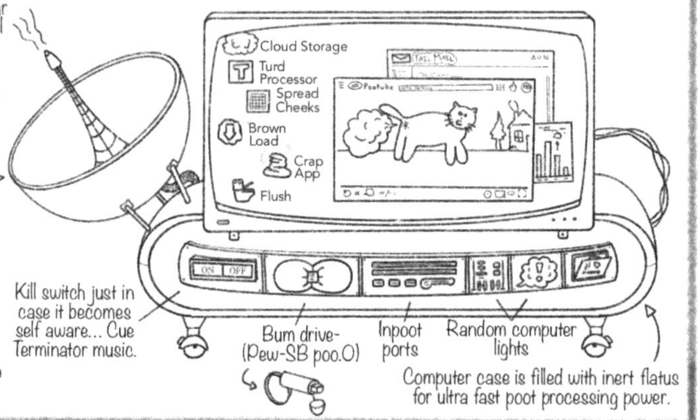

Model:
Craptop

This computer is just like a regular laptop except it only performs fart related functions...and costs twice as much.

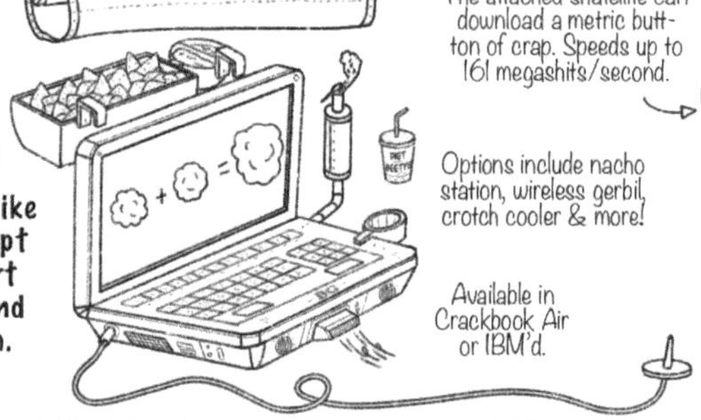

Colon Codes

This colon clang calculator blurts out some pretty crazy gas-trick bypasses. Great for your next 'yo mama' insult battle!

Here's a look into the genius of our colon coders crusty computations. Discover computer generated flatulence phrases, simulated stink sounds, reek reactions, acrid acronyms and more! They come out with new crap all the time.

Acrid Acronyms

Generate accurate acronyms for any fart related word.

Forced	Tumultuous
Actuated	Oust
Rectal	Of
Tremor	Taradiddle
Fine	Torrential
Anal	Odor
Reverberating	Outpour
Trebuchet	Tunnel
Focused	Forced
Acute	Lower
Rear	Air
Turret	Trickle
Frisky	Underwear
Air	Stink
Response	Gross
Tantrum	Anal
Foul	Sneeze
Amplified	Generate
Raunchy	Asphyxiating
Trama	Stench

Onomatopoeia IKEA

Mix & match the columns

HUOR	UURR	TFFT	ARFT
FLAA	AHHR	PFFU	OUFP
EIEI	YIRF	EEEE	LIIP
RRII	BRUU	DURH	HURM
QQQU	UUEE	UUHL	EFFF
MEEE	OUFT	AASS	UHHG
SSCS	OIIA	RUUO	IIUS

Rancid Rhymes

You toot, it computes...

Straining too hard equals,
Raining poo shards.

Whoever reeks from behind,
Freely speaks their mind.

A toot scoot is fun but,
Toot loot means you need to run.

Thunder of brown wonder, makes
Plunder from down under.

Full of linger, please
Pull my finger.

A drop must rust,
for cropdust to crust.

Brew pew stew, with
New poo rue.

Your backside surely supplied it,
But your topside sorely denied it.
Your inside prematurely decried it,
And now your outside purely can't hide it.

Brown Sounds to Nouns

Add words together to describe the ultimate fart

Mood	Start	Middle	Finish
Steady	Machine gun	Free flow	Fizzle out
Raising pitch	Whisper	Motor boat	Squeal
Lowering pitch	Pop	Croaking	Rasp
Raising tone	Blast	Oozing	Groan
Lowering tone	Squeak	Backfire	Dump
Wavering	Gurgling	Screeching	Shart

Fart Phrases

Pick a number between 1 & 15, 4 times: __,__,__,__.
Then read the corresponding word from each column.
(Add a, an or some between columns 1 & 2).

1	Blast	Really	Stinky	Fart
2	Rip	Very	Thick	Shart
3	Let	Extra	Petite	Toot
4	Squeeze	Extremely	Mammoth	Blast
5	Force	Exceptionally	King-sized	Breeze
6	Flatulate	Especially	Extended	Butt Burp
7	Cut	Legitimately	Juicy	Gas
8	Pop	Categorically	Disgusting	Poot
9	Expel	Indubitably	Windy	Flatus
10	Pass	Authentically	Delicious	Barking Spider
11	Eject	Certainly	Squeaky	Fluff
12	Oust	Honestly	Silent	Erutation
13	Discharge	Truly	Wet	Speaker
14	Deport	Admittedly	Abrupt	Wind
15	Evict	Terribly	Dank	SBD

Fart Reaction Generator

Pick one phrase from each set of brackets, then read the sentence.

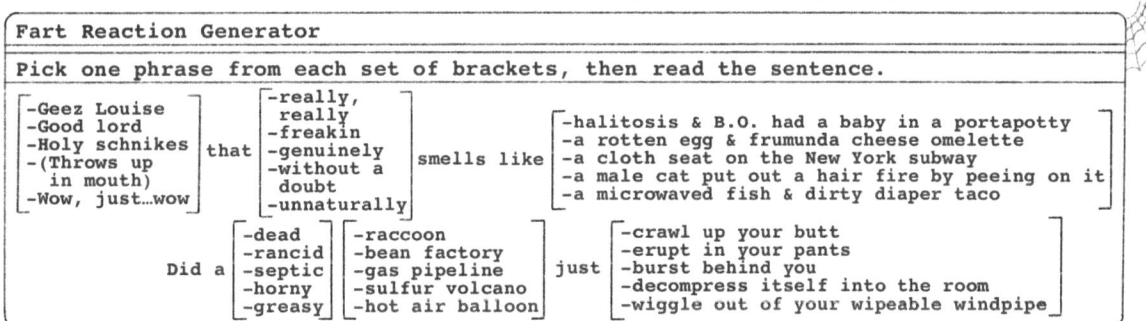

Crappy Careers

Ever thought of turning your excessive flatulence into a full blown pooting profession? That's right, get paid to cut the proverbial cheese. Maybe become a gasologist, smelectrician or fartriloquist! Find out if you've got what it takes; call our toot recruit center today!

Gassassin

Learn to be as silent and deadly as an SBD in our Flying Buttress Ninja Academy.

Earn various fart color related belts in Bung-Poo Kung-Fu, Poo Shitsu and Crapkido.

Master weapons such as the backside blow gun, bumchucks, butt sais, stink stars & more.

Church of Flatus

Become a deplordained minister of the Lurch Church. A place where all are welcome to supply it, and no one has to deny it.

Give stink sermons, perform craptisms, and pray for spray.

Eat, drink and be gassy!

Derrière Ride Share

There are plenty of "regular" taxis out there, but now you can share rides and stink! (Editor: Remove line before publishing) We own several competing companies to make it seem like consumers have a choice.

Be smelt, but not seen! Fulfill your dustiny; become a master Cropduster.

Learn classic tales like:
Adam & Relieve: The Forbidden Toot
The Blast Supper: Brussel Sprout Betrayal
Moses Farts the Red Sea

Bring your own stink mobile!

Fartist

You've heard the term artsy fartsy before. Let the creativity flow out of you!

Learn all the digestive gas related arts: Pants Dance, Taint Paint, [gl]ass blowing & more.

Air-obics Instructor

Become a professional worker outer... of farts that is.

Get ripped while let 'em rip!

Fart DJ

MC StinkyPantz, DJ Air Biscuits, Sir Shitzalot. Learn to float the notes from the goats!

Brown Cloud Spa

Help provide a luxurious relaxing experience for people who also have a fartesian fart fetish.

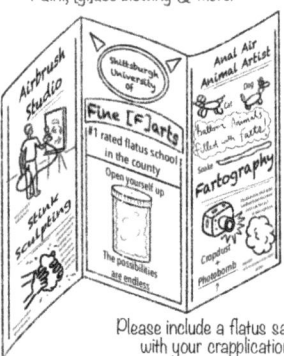

Please include a flatus sample with your crapplication.

Become the master blaster of all gas genie related exercises.

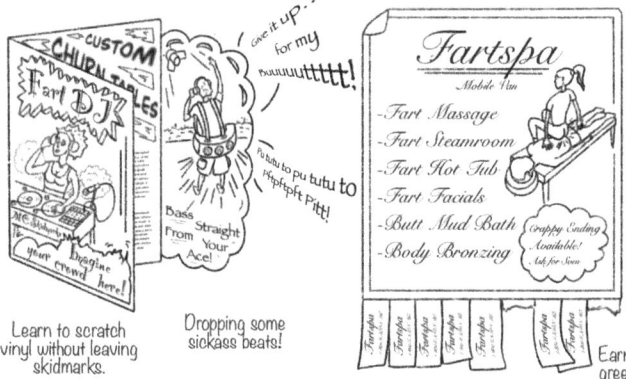

Learn to scratch vinyl without leaving skidmarks.

Dropping some sickass beats!

Earn your green and brown card!

www.ingramcontent.com/pod-product-compliance
Lightning Source LLC
Chambersburg PA
CBHW061402010526
44119CB00010B/233